The Real Thing

Henry James (1843 - 1916) was born in New York. His family was very talented: his father and brother were important philosophers. His education took place in New York and later in London, Paris and Geneva, and finally at Harvard Law School in 1862. He began writing reviews and short stories in 1864 and in 1875 moved to Paris for a year, then to London and finally in 1898 to a house in the English countryside. His reputation is based on his novels *(including such famous ones as "The Europeans", "The Portrait of a Lady", "The Bostonians", "The Ambassadors")* but also on his short stories, a form which he treated masterfully. The story in this volume was first published in 1893. Henry James was always attracted to Europe and the different sensibility of the *"Old World"* and became a naturalised British citizen in 1915, a year before his death in London.

La Spiga

THE REAL THING

1

WHEN the porter's wife (she used to answer the house-bell), announced 'A gentleman - with a lady, sir,' I had, as I often had in those days, for the wish was father to the thought, an immediate vision of sitters. Sitters my visitors in this case proved to be; but not in the sense I should have preferred. However, there was nothing at first to indicate that they might not have come for a portrait. The gentleman, a man of fifty, very high and very straight, with a moustache slightly grizzled and a dark grey wailking-coat admirably fitted, both of which I noted professionally - I don't mean as a barber or yet as a tailor - would have struck me as a celebrity if celebrities often were striking. It was a truth of which I had for some time been conscious that a figure with a good deal of frontage was, as one might say,

porter: person looking after a house, admitting visitors etc.
house-bell: bell to call servants.

the wish was father to the thought: his wish made him assume sitters had arrived. **Sitters**: people posing for paintings, models.
proved to be: in fact were.
portrait: painting of a person.
straight: not curved.
slightly: a little. **grizzled**: grey. **walking-coat**: type of clothes.
admirably: very well. **fitted**: cut, made.
barber: someone who cuts hair. **tailor**: someone who makes clothes. **struck me**: made me think. **celebrity**: famous person.
striking: conspicuous.
good deal: lot. **frontage**: fine appearance.

almost never a public institution. A glance at the lady helped to remind me of this paradoxical law: she also looked too distinguished to be a 'personality'. Moreover one would scarcely come across two variations together. Neither of the pair spoke immediately - they only prolonged the preliminary gaze which suggested that each wished to give the other a chance. They were visibly shy; they stood there letting me take them in - which, as I afterwards perceived, was the most practical thing they could have done. In this way their embarrassment served their cause. I had seen people painfully reluctant to mention that they desired anything so gross as to be represented on canvas; but the scruples of my new friends appeared almost insurmountable. Yet the gentleman might have said 'I should like a portrait of my wife', and the lady might have said 'I should like a portrait of my husband'. Perhaps they were not husband and wife - this naturally would make the matter more delicate. Perhaps they wished to be done together - in which case they ought to have brought a third person to break the news.

'We come from Mr Rivet,' the lady said at last, with a dim smile which had the effect of a moist sponge passed over a 'sunk' piece of painting, as well as of a vague allusion to vanished beauty. She was as tall and straight, in her degree, as her companion, and with ten years less to carry. She looked as sad as a woman could look whose face was not charged with expression; that is her tinted oval mask showed friction as an exposed surface shows it. The hand of

glance: quick look.
remind me: make me remember. **paradoxical**: contradictory.
distinguished: refined. **Moreover**: in addition.
scarcely: almost never. **come across**: meet.
pair: two.
prolonged: continued. **gaze**: long look.
wished: wanted. **visibly**: clearly. **shy**: timid.
letting me take them in: letting me observe them and make a judgement. **perceived**: realised.
served their cause: helped them in what they wanted to do.
painfully: extremely, to the point of displeasure. **reluctant**: not wanting to do something. **mention**: say. **desired**: wanted.
gross: vulgar. **represented on canvas**: painted. **scruples**: moral principles. **insurmountable**: impossible to overcome.
Yet: but. **portrait**: painting, picture.

matter: situation. **wished**: wanted.
ought to: should.
break the news: tell the painter what they wanted.
dim: not strong.
moist: damp, wet. **sponge**: soft cloth used for cleaning.
'sunk': without colour. **vague**: unclear. **allusion**: reference.
vanished: disappeared. **degree**: posture
with ten years less to carry: she was ten years younger.

charged with: full of. **tinted**: coloured. **oval**: shaped like an egg.
friction: tension. **exposed**: open to observation.

time had played over her freely, but only to simplify. She was slim and stiff, and so well dressed, in dark blue cloth, with lappets and pockets and buttons, that it was clear she employed the same tailor as her husband. The couple had an indefinable air of prosperous thrift - they evidently got a good deal of luxury for their money. If I was to be one of their luxuries it would behove me to consider my terms.

'Ah, Claude Rivet recommended me,' I inquired; and I added that it was very kind of him, though I could reflect that, as he only painted landscape, this was not a sacrifice. The lady looked very hard at the gentleman, and the gentleman looked round the room. Then staring at the floor a moment and stroking his moustache, he rested his pleasant eyes on me with the remark: 'He said you were the right one.'

'I try to be, when people want to sit.'

'Yes, we should like to,' said the lady anxiously.

'Do you mean together?'

My visitors exchanged a glance. 'If you could do anything with *me*, I suppose it would be double,' the gentleman stammered.

'Oh yes, there's naturally a higher charge for two figures than for one.'

'We would like to make it pay,' the husband confessed.

'That's very good of you,' I returned, appreciating so unwonted a sympathy - for I supposed he meant pay the artist. A sense of strangeness seemed to dawn on the lady. 'We mean for the illustrations - Mr Rivet said you might put one in.'

The hand of time had played over her freely: there were many signs of her age on her face. **slim**: not fat or robust. **stiff**: rigid, formal. **cloth**: material. **lappets**: folds of cloth.
employed: used. **tailor**: person making clothes. **couple**: two people. **indefinable**: which could not be defined. **prosperous**: successful, with money. **thrift**: not spending their money in a stupid way. **a good deal of**: a lot of. **luxury**: expensive things.
it would behove me: I should. **inquired**: asked.
though: even if. **reflect**: think.
landscape: views of natural scenes.
hard: intensely.
staring: looking.
stroking: caressing. **moustache**: facial hair above mouth. **rested**: put. **remark**: something said.

sit: model, pose.
anxiously: in an agitated way.

exchanged a glance: looked at each other.
it: the cost.
stammered: said in a hesitating way.
higher: more expensive. **charge**: cost.

unwonted: unusual. **meant**: intended.
dawn: begin to appear.

'Put one in - an illustration?' I was equally confused.

'Sketch her off, you know,' said the gentleman, colouring. It was only then that I understood the service Claude Rivet had rendered me; he had told them that I worked in black and white, for magazines, for story-books, for sketches of contemporary life, and consequently had frequent employment for models. These things were true, but it was not less true (I may confess it now - whether because the aspiration was to lead to everything or to nothing I leave the reader to guess), that I couldn't get the honours, to say nothing of the emoluments, of a great painter of portraits out of my head. My 'illustrations' were my pot-boilers; I looked to a different branch of art (far and away the most interesting it had always seemed to me), to perpetuate my fame. There was no shame in looking to it also to make my fortune; but that fortune was by so much further from being made from the moment my visitors wished to be 'done' for nothing. I was disappointed, for in the pictorial sense I had immediately *seen* them. I had seized their type - I had already settled what I would do with it. Something that wouldn't absolutely have pleased them, I afterwards reflected.

'Ah, you're - you're - a - ?' I began, as soon as I had mastered my surprise. I couldn't bring out the dingy word 'models'; it seemed to fit the case so little.

'We haven't had much practice,' said the lady.

'We've got to *do* something, and we've thought that an artist in your line might perhaps make something of us,'

Sketch: do a quick drawing. **colouring**: becoming red in the face from emotion.

sketches: quick drawings.
consequently: so.

whether: if.
aspiration: ambition.

emoluments: money asked for paintings. **portraits**: paintings of people. **pot-boilers**: books written only for money.
branch: sector. **far and away**: most certainly.
perpetuate: prolong, make something last for ever.
shame: embarrassment. **it**: the illustrations.
fortune: lots of money, financial success. **by so much**: a lot.
further from being made: less probable. **wished**: wanted.
disappointed: unhappy.
seized: understood immediately.
settled: decided.
pleased them: made them happy.
reflected: thought.

mastered: dominated. **bring out**: say. **dingy**: depressing.
fit: be appropriate to.

her husband threw off. He further mentioned that they didn't know many artists and that they had gone first, on the off-chance (he painted views of course, but sometimes put in figures - perhaps I remembered), to Mr Rivet, whom they had met a few years before at a place in Norfolk where he was sketching.

'We used to sketch a little ourselves,' the lady hinted.

'It's very awkward, but we absolutely *must* do something,' her husband went on.

'Of course, we're not so *very* young,' she admitted, with a wan smile.

With the remark that I might as well know something more about them, the husband had handed me a card extracted from a neat new pocket-book (their appurtenances were all of the freshest) and inscribed with the words 'Major Monarch'. Impressive as these words were they didn't carry my knowledge much further; but my visitor presently added: 'I've left the army, and we've had the misfortune to lose our money. In fact our means are dreadfully small.'

'It's an awful bore,' said Mrs Monarch.

They evidently wished to be discreet - to take care not to swagger because they were gentlefolks. I perceived they would have been willing to recognize this as something of a drawback, at the same time that I guessed at an underlying sense - their consolation in adversity - that they *had* their points. They certainly had; but these advantages struck me as preponderantly social; such for instance as

threw off: said casually.

on the off-chance: casually. **views**: paintings of nature.

Norfolk: region in the East of England.
sketching: making drawings.
hinted: suggested.
awkward: embarrassing, inconvenient.

wan: pale, unenthusiastic.
might as well: could not lose anything by.
handed: given.
neat: tidy, orderly. **pocket-book**: wallet. **appurtenances**: accessories. **freshest**: newest.
Impressive: making a good impression.
carry my knowledge much further: let me know any more.
presently: soon.
misfortune: bad luck. **means**: money and property. **dreadfully**: terribly.
awful: terrible. **bore**: something boring or uninteresting.
evidently: obviously. **wished**: wanted. **discreet**: polite.
swagger: be arrogant. **gentlefolks**: of high social status. **perceived**: understood. **willing**: prepared.
drawback: disadvantage.
underlying: hidden, under the surface. **consolation**: compensation. **adversity**: difficult circumstances. ***had* their points**: had their advantages. **struck me**: seemed to me. **preponderantly**: mostly. **for instance**: for example.

11

would help to make a drawing-room look well. However, a drawing-room was always, or ought to be, a picture.

In consequence of his wife's allusion to their age Major Monarch observed: 'Naturally, it's more for the figure that we thought of going in. We can still hold ourselves up.' On the instant I saw that the figure was indeed their strong point. His 'naturally' didn't sound vain, but it lighted up the question. '*She* has got the best,' he continued, nodding at his wife, with a pleasant after-dinner absence of circumlocution. I could only reply, as if we were in fact sitting over our wine, that this didn't prevent his own from being very good; which led him in turn to rejoin: 'We thought that if you ever have to do people like us, we might be something like it. *She*, particularly - for a lady in a book, you know.'

I was so amused by them that, to get more of it, I did my best to take their point of view; and though it was an embarrassment to find myself appraising physically, as if they were animals on hire or useful blacks, a pair of whom I should have expected to meet only in one of the relations in which criticism is tacit, I looked at Mrs Monarch judicially enough to be able to exclaim, after a moment, with conviction: 'Oh yes, a lady in a book!' She was singularly like a bad illustration.

'We'll stand up, if you like,' said the Major; and he raised himself before me with a really grand air.

I could take his measure at a glance - he was six feet two and a perfect gentleman. It would have paid any club in

drawing-room: room where visitors were formally received.
ought to: should.
In consequence of: following. **allusion**: reference.
figure: their posture and appearance.
going in: trying modelling.
instant: moment.
strong point: best characteristic. **vain**: proud.

nodding at: indicating with his head.
absence of circumlocution: directness.
his own: the man's figure.
led: caused. **rejoin**: reply.

amused: pleasantly stimulated.

appraising: evaluating.
on hire: to be rented. **blacks**: black servants.

criticism is tacit: criticism is thought but not said.
judicially: with judgement.
conviction: state of being convinced. **singularly**: unusually.

raised himself: stood up. **grand**: important air. appearance.
take his measure: decide how tall he was. **six feet two**: about 1 metre 88 cm. **have paid**: have been an advantage to.

process of formation and in want of a stamp to engage him at a salary to stand in the principal window. What struck me immediately was that in coming to me they had rather missed their vocation; they could surely have been turned to better account for advertising purposes. I couldn't of course see the thing in detail, but I could see them make someone's fortune - I don't mean their own. There was something in them for a waistcoat-maker, an hotel-keeper, or a soap-vendor. I could imagine 'We always use it' pinned on their bosoms with the greatest effect; I had a vision of the promptitude with which they would launch a *table d'hôte*.

Mrs Monarch sat still, not from pride but from shyness, and presently her husband said to her: 'Get up my dear and show how smart you are.' She obeyed, but she had no need to get up to show it. She walked to the end of the studio, and then she came back blushing, with her fluttered eyes on her husband. I was reminded of an incident I had accidentally had a glimpse of in Paris - being with a friend there, a dramatist about to produce a play - when an actress came to him to ask to be intrusted with a part. She went through the paces before him, walked up and down as Mrs Monarch was doing. Mrs Monarch did it quite as well, but I abstained from applauding. It was very odd to see such people apply for such poor pay. She looked as if she had ten thousand a year. Her husband had used the word that described her: she was, in the London current jargon, essentially and typically 'smart'. Her figure was, in the

in want of a stamp: needing a particular character. **engage**: employ. **struck**: affected.
rather: a little.
missed their vocation: chosen the wrong job.
turned to better account: used more profitably. **purposes**: aims.
fortune: financial success.
waistcoat-maker: person making an item of clothing worn under a jacket. **soap-vendor**: person selling soap.
pinned: attached. **bosoms**: chests.
promptitude: skill. **launch**: promote.
table d'hôte: fixed menu *(French)*.
pride: self-regard. **shyness**: timidity.
presently: soon.
smart: elegant. **obeyed**: did what she was told.

blushing: red from emotion. **fluttered**: opening and shutting quickly. **I was reminded**: it made me remember. **incident**: event. **had a glimpse of**: see a little of.
dramatist: person writing for the theatre.
intrusted with: given. **a part**: a role in a play.
went through the paces: showed him what she could do.

abstained from applauding: did not clap my hands. **odd**: strange. **apply**: ask for a job. **poor**: little.
ten thousand a year: ten thousand pounds a year of private income, a lot of money in those days. **jargon**: informal speech.
'smart': elegant.

same order of ideas, conspicuously and irreproachably 'good'. For a woman of her age her waist was surprisingly small; her elbow moreover had the orthodox crook. She held her head at the conventional angle; but why did she come to *me*? She ought to have tried on jackets at a big shop. I feared my visitors were not only destitute, but 'artistic' - which would be a great complication. When she sat down again I thanked her, observing that what a draughtsman most valued in his model was the faculty of keeping quiet.

'Oh, *she* can keep quiet,' said Major Monarch. Then he added, jocosely: 'I've always kept her quiet.'

'I'm not a nasty fidget, am I?' Mrs Monarch appealed to her husband.

He addressed his answer to me. 'Perhaps it isn't out of place to mention - because we ought to be quite businesslike, oughtn't we? - that when I married her she was known as the Beautiful Statue.'

'Oh dear!' said Mrs Monarch, ruefully.

'Of course I should want a certain amount of expression,' I rejoined.

'Of *course*!' they both exclaimed.

'And then I suppose you know that you'll get awfully tired.'

'Oh, we *never* get tired!' they eagerly cried.

'Have you had any kind of practice?'

They hesitated - they looked at each other. 'We've been photographed, *immensely*,' said Mrs Monarch.

irreproachably: could not be criticised.

waist: middle of body.

elbow: joint in middle of arm. **moreover**: in addition. **orthodox**: standard, normal. **crook**: curve. **angle**: position.

ought to: should. **tried on jackets**: demonstrated clothes to customers. **feared**: was afraid. **destitute**: poor.

draughtsman: someone who draws. **faculty**: ability.

jocosely: laughing, in a joking manner.

nasty: unpleasant. **fidget**: someone who cannot remain stationary. **appealed to**: asked with emotion.

addressed: directed.

mention: say. **ought to**: should.

businesslike: professional.

ruefully: sadly.

amount: quantity.

rejoined: replied.

awfully: terribly.

eagerly: with enthusiasm.

hesitated. paused to think.

immensely: a lot.

'She means the fellows have asked us,' added the Major.
'I see - because you're so good-looking.'
'I don't know what they thought, but they were always after us.'
'We always got our photographs for nothing,' smiled Mrs Monarch.
'We might have brought some, my dear,' her husband remarked.
'I'm not sure we have any left. We've given quantities away,'
she explained to me.
'With our autographs and that sort of thing,' said the Major.
'Are they to be got in the shops?' I inquired, as a harmless pleasantry.
'Oh, yes; *hers* - they used to be.'
'Not now,' said Mrs Monarch, with her eyes on the floor.

2

I could fancy the 'sort of thing' they put on the presentation-copies of their photographs, and I was sure they wrote a beautiful hand. It was odd how quickly I was sure of everything that concerned them. If they were now so poor as to have to earn shillings and pence, they never had had much of a margin. Their good looks had been their capital, and they had good-humouredly made the most of the

fellows: men.

might: should.

left: remaining.
given quantities away: given lots to other people.

autographs: signatures.

got: bought. **inquired**: asked. **harmless**: innocuous.
pleasantry: piece of polite conversation.

fancy: imagine.

beautiful hand: good handwriting **odd**: strange.
concerned: involved.
earn: get money for a job. **shillings and pence**: until 1971 the pound sterling was divided into 20 shillings, each of 12 pence.
margin: money to spend on unnecessary things. **good-humouredly**: in a pleasant way. **made the most of**: taken as much advantage as possible of.

career that this resource marked out for them. It was in their faces, the blankness, the deep intellectual repose of the twenty years of country-house visiting which had given them pleasant intonations. I could see the sunny drawing-rooms, sprinkled with periodicals she didn't read, in which Mrs Monarch had continuously sat; I could see the wet shrubberies in which she had walked, equipped to admiration for either exercise. I could see the rich covers the Major had helped to shoot and the wonderful garments in which, late at night, he repaired to the smoking-room to talk about them. I could imagine their leggings and waterproofs, their knowing tweeds and rugs, their rolls of sticks and cases of tackle and neat umbrellas; and I could evoke the exact appearance of their servants and the compact variety of their luggage on the platforms of country stations.

They gave small tips, but they were liked; they didn't do anything themselves, but they were welcome. They looked so well everywhere; they gratified the general relish for stature, complexion, and 'form'. They knew it without fatuity or vulgarity, and they respected themselves in consequence. They were not superficial; they were thorough and kept themselves up - it had been their line. People with such a taste for activity had to have some line. I could feel how, even in a dull house, they could have been counted upon for cheerfulness. At present something had happened - it didn't matter what, their little income had grown less, it had grown least - and they had to do some-

resource: characteristic. **marked out**: indicated.

blankness: emptiness. **repose**: rest.

country-house: rich people's houses in the country.

intonations: way of speaking.

drawing-room: room where visitors were formally received.

sprinkled: covered lightly. **periodicals**: newspapers and magazines. **wet**: damp, covered with water. **shrubberies**: low trees.

equipped: having characteristics and looks. **either exercise**: sitting indoors or walking outdoors. **covers**: carpets and other coverings, here made from animals or birds. **shoot**: kill with a gun.

garments: clothes. **repaired**: retired. **leggings**: coverings worn on legs during hunting. **waterproofs**: clothes which did not let water in. **knowing**: well-chosen. **tweeds**: clothes made of a particular kind of wool. **rugs**: carpets. **rolls of sticks and cases of tackle**: utensils for hunting and fishing. **neat**: tidy. **evoke**: imagine. **luggage**: suitcases.

tips: gratuities, money given to servants if they do a good job.

gratified: satisfied. **relish**: taste.

stature: imposing figures. **complexion**: type.

fatuity: stupidity, obvious things.

thorough: meticulous, careful about everything. **kept themselves up**: maintained themselves in society. **line**: typical behaviour. **dull**: boring.

counted upon: relied on. **cheerfulness**: happiness.

income: money.

thing for pocket-money. Their friends liked them, but didn't like to support them. There was something about them that represented credit - their clothes, their manners, their type; but if credit is a large empty pocket in which an occasional chink reverberates, the chink at least must be audible. What they wanted of me was to help to make it so. Fortunately they had no children - I soon divined that. They would also perhaps wish our relations to be kept secret: this was why it was 'for the figure' - the reproduction of the face would betray them.

I liked them - they were so simple; and I had no objection to them if they would suit. But, somehow, with all their perfections I didn't easily believe in them. After all they were amateurs, and the ruling passion of my life was the detestation of the amateur. Combined with this was another perversity - an innate preference for the represented subject over the real one: the defect of the real one was so apt to be a lack of representation. I liked things that appeared; then one was sure. Whether they *were* or not was a subordinate and almost always a profitless question. There were other considerations, the first of which was that I already had two or three people in use, notably a young person with big feet, in alpaca, from Kilburn, who for a couple of years had come to me regularly for my illustrations and with whom I was still - perhaps ignobly - satisfied. I frankly explained to my visitors how the case stood; but they had taken more precautions than I supposed. They had reasoned out their opportunity, for Claude

pocket-money: money to spend on personal pleasures.

chink: sound of money. **reverberates**: vibrates, sounds.
audible: able to be heard. **to make it so**: *(here)* to give them some money. **Fortunately**: luckily. **divined**: guessed, discovered.
wish: want.
'for the figure': body. **reproduction**: painting or drawing.
betray: make their secret public.

suit: be appropriate. **somehow**: in some way.

amateurs: not professionals. **ruling**: most important.
detestation: hating.
perversity: strange behaviour. **innate**: natural. **represented**: painted, artificial. **defect**: negative characteristic.
apt: probable. **lack of representation**: not enough represenation.
subordinate: less important. **profitless**: without advantage.

notably: particularly.
alpaca: type of woollen clothes. **Kilburn**: suburb of London.

illuctrations: drawings. **ignobly**: opposite of nobly.
frankly: honestly, sincerely.
the case stood: things were.
reasoned: thought carefully.

23

Rivet had told them of the projected *édition de luxe* of one of the writers of our day - the rarest of the novelists - who, long neglected by the multitudinous vulgar and dearly prized by the attentive (need I mention Philip Vincent?) had had the happy fortune of seeing, late in life, the dawn and then the full light of a higher criticism - an estimate in which, on the part of the public, there was something really of expiation. The edition in question, planned by a publisher of taste, was practically an act of high reparation; the woodcuts with which it was to be enriched were the homage of English art to one of the most independent representatives of English letters. Major and Mrs Monarch confessed to me that they had hoped I might be able to work *them* into my share of the enterprise. They knew I was to do the first of the books, *Rutland Ramsay,* but I had to make clear to them that my participation in the rest of the affair- this first book was to be a test - was to depend on the satisfaction I should give. If this should be limited my employers would drop me without a scruple. It was therefore a crisis for me, and naturally I was making special preparation, looking about for new people, if they should be necessary, and securing the best types. I admitted however that I should like to settle down to two or three good models who would do for everything.

'Should we have often to - a - put on special clothes?' Mrs Monarch timidly demanded.

'Dear, yes - that's half the business.'

'And should we be expected to supply our own costumes?'

projected: planned. ***édition de luxe:*** luxury, high-quality edition.
rarest: most refined.
neglected: ignored. **multitudinous**: many.
prized: valued, regarded. **attentive**: careful.
fortune: luck, destiny. **dawn**: start.
estimate: evaluation.

expiation: penitence for something wrong, the public was sorry it had neglected the writer for so long. **of taste**: refined. **reparation**: compensation for something wrong. **woodcuts**: type of illustrations. **enriched**: decorated. **homage**: tribute.
letters: writing.
confessed: admitted.
share: part. **enterprise**: project.

drop me: not use any more of my work. **scruple**: moral problem.
therefore: for this reason. **crisis**: important moment.

securing: making sure of.
settle down: stabilise, choose definitively.
do: be acceptable.

demanded: asked.
half the business: very important in this work.
supply: bring, provide.

'Oh, no; I've got a lot of things. A painter's models put on - or put off - anything he likes.'

'And do you mean - a - the same?'

'The same?'

Mrs Monarch looked at her husband again.

'Oh, she was just wondering,' he explained, 'if the costumes are in *general* use.' I had to confess that they were, and I mentioned further that some of them (I had a lot of genuine, greasy last-century things) had served their time, a hundred years ago, on living, world-stained men and women. 'We'll put on anything that *fits*,' said the Major.

'Oh, I arrange that - they fit in the pictures.'

'I'm afraid I should do better for the modern books. I would come as you like,' said Mrs Monarch.

'She has got a lot of clothes at home: they might do for contemporary life,' her husband continued.

'Oh, I can fancy scenes in which you'd be quite natural.' And indeed I could see the slipshod rearrangements of stale properties - the stories I tried to produce pictures for without the exasperation of reading them - whose sandy tracts the good lady might help to people. But I had to return to the fact that for this sort of work - the daily mechanical grind - I was already equipped, the people I was working with were fully adequate.

'We only thought we might be more like *some* characters,' said Mrs Monarch mildly, getting up.

Her husband also rose; he stood looking at me with a dim wistfulness that was touching in so fine a man. 'Wouldn't

wondering: asking herself, speculating.

general **use**: worn by many people. **confess**: admit.

mentioned: said. **further**: in addition.

genuine: real. **greasy**: a little dirty. **served their time**: been used. **world-stained**: real, with the marks of living.

fits: is the right size, is suitable.

arrange: organize.

I'm afraid: I think.

might do: might be acceptable.

contemporary: present-day.

fancy: imagine.

slipshod: poor quality.

stale: old. **properties**: clothes and other accessories for a picture. **exasperation**: irritation. **sandy**: covered with sand.

tracts: spaces. **people**: fill.

daily: everyday.

grind: unpleasant work. **equipped**: provided with models.

mildly: softly.

rose: got up. **dim**: faint, not intense.

wistfulness: sense of regret or nostalgia, delicate sadness. **touching**: had an effect on the emotions.

it be rather a pull sometimes to have - a - to have - ?' He hung fire; he wanted me to help him by phrasing what he meant. But I couldn't - I didn't know. So he brought it out, awkwardly: 'The *real* thing; a gentleman, you know, or a lady.' I was quite ready to give a general assent - I admitted that there was a great deal in that. This encouraged Major Monarch to say, following up his appeal with an unacted gulp: 'It's awfully hard - we've tried everything.' The gulp was communicative; it proved too much for his wife. Before I knew it Mrs Monarch had dropped again upon a divan and burst into tears. Her husband sat down beside her, holding one of her hands; whereupon she quickly dried her eyes with the other, while I felt embarrassed as she looked up at me. 'There isn't a confounded job I haven't applied for - waited for - prayed for. You can fancy we'd be pretty bad at first. Secretaryships and that sort of thing? You might as well ask for a peerage. I'd be *anything* - I'm strong; a messenger or a coalheaver. I'd put on a gold-laced cap and open carriage doors in front of the haberdasher's; I'd hang about a station, to carry portmanteaux; I'd be a postman. But they won't *look* at you; there are thousands, as good as yourself, already on the ground. *Gentlemen*, poor beggars, who have drunk their wine, who have kept their hunters!'

I was as reassuring as I knew how to be, and my visitors were presently on their feet again while, for the experiment, we agreed on an hour. We were discussing it when the door opened and Miss Churm came in with a wet

rather a pull: quite an attraction. **hung fire**: paused. **phrasing**: putting into words.

meant: intended.

awkwardly: not elegantly.

give a general assent: say yes in general.

a great deal: a lot of truth.

appeal: request. **unacted**: real, genuine.

gulp: sound in throat. **awfully**: terribly. **hard**: difficult.

communicative: expressive. **proved**: was.

dropped: fallen.

burst into tears: suddenly started crying.

whereupon: when.

confounded: damned.

applied for: written to ask for. **fancy**: imagine.

pretty: quite. **Secretaryships**: the post of secretary.

peerage: to be a lord.

coalheaver: person moving coal, a solid black fuel.

gold-laced: decorated with gold. **carriage**: horse vehicle.

haberdasher's: shop selling men'sclothes. **hang about**: wait at.

portmanteaux: type of suitcase.

on the ground: in existence.

beggars: people without money.

reassuring: comforting.

presently: soon.

umbrella. Miss Churm had to take the omnibus to Maida Vale and then walk half a mile. She looked a trifle blowsy and slightly splashed. I scarcely ever saw her come in without thinking afresh how odd it was that, being so little in herself, she should yet be so much in others. She was a meagre little Miss Churm, but she was an ample heroine of romance. She was only a freckled cockney, but she could represent everything from a fine lady to a shepherdess; she had the faculty, as she might have had a fine voice or long hair. She couldn't spell, and she loved beer, but she had two or three 'points', and practice, and a knack, and mother-wit, and a kind of whimsical sensibility, and a love of the theatre, and seven sisters, and not an ounce of respect, especially for the 'h'. The first thing my visitors saw was that her umbrella was wet, and in their spotless perfection they visibly winced at it. The rain had come on since their arrival.

'I'm all in a soak; there *was* a mess of people in the bus. I wish you lived near a station,' said Miss Churm. I requested her to get ready as quickly as possible, and she passed into the room in which she always changed her dress. But before going out she asked me what she was to get into this time.

'It's the Russian princess, don't you know?' I answered; 'the one with the "golden eyes", in black velvet, for the long thing in the *Cheapside*.'

'Golden eyes? I *say!*' cried Miss Churm, while my companions watched her with intensity as she withdrew. She

omnibus: public transport.

half a mile: about 800 metres. **trifle**: little. **blowsy**: vulgar. **slightly**: a little. **splashed**: marked by the water. **scarcely ever**: almost never. **afresh**: again. **odd**: strange.

meagre: thin. **ample**: substantial.

freckled: with marks on the skin. **cockney**: person from London.

shepherdess: woman looking after sheep.

faculty: ability.

'points': good characteristics. **knack**: ability.

mother-wit: natural intelligence. **whimsical**: playful. **sensibility**: feelings. **ounce**: about 30 grams, a very small quantity.

'h': London people do not aspirate 'h'.

spotless: without marks.

winced: made a shocked movement. **come on**: started.

soak: wet. **mess**: crowd, confusion.

what she was to get into: what costume she should put on.

velvet: soft material.

Cheapside: magazine.

I *say!*: exclamation, marvellous!

withdrew: went to change.

always arranged herself, when she was late, before I could turn round; and I kept my visitors a little, on purpose, so that they might get an idea, from seeing her, what would be expected of themselves. I mentioned that she was quite my notion of an excellent model - she was really very clever.

'Do you think she looks like a Russian princess?' Major Monarch asked, with lurking alarm.

'When I make her, yes.'

'Oh, if you have to *make* her - !' He reasoned, acutely.

'That's the most you can ask. There are so many that are not makeable.'

'Well now, *here's* a lady' - and with a persuasive smile he passed his arm into his wife's - 'who's already made!'

'Oh, I'm not a Russian princess,' Mrs Monarch protested, a little coldly. I could see that she had known some and didn't like them. There, immediately, was a complication of a kind that I never had to fear with Miss Churm.

This young lady came back in black velvet - the gown was rather rusty and very low on her lean shoulders - and with a Japanese fan in her red hands. I reminded her that in the scene I was doing she had to look over someone's head. 'I forget whose it is; but it doesn't matter. Just look over a head.'

'I'd rather look over a stove,' said Miss Churm; and she took her station near the fire. She fell into position, settled herself into a tall attitude, gave a certain backward inclination to her head and a certain forward drop to her fan, and

arranged: organized.
on purpose: deliberately.

mentioned: said. **quite**: exactly.
notion: idea.
clever: skilful.

lurking: a suspicion of. **alarm**: fear.

reasoned: thought logically. **acutely**: intelligently.

are not makeable: cannot be made into anything.

some: that is some princesses.

fear: be afraid of.
gown: dress.
rusty: old. **lean**: thin. **shoulders**: upper part of back.
fan: instrument for ventilation. **reminded**: told.

rathor: prcfcr to. **stove**: healer.
station: pocition. **octtled**: arranged.
attitude: posture.
inclination: curve. **drop**: downward movement. **fan**: insturment for ventilation.

33

looked, at least to my prejudiced sense, distinguished and charming, foreign and dangerous. We left her looking so, while I went downstairs with Major and Mrs Monarch.

'I think I could come about as near it as that,' said Mrs Monarch.

'Oh, you think she's shabby, but you must allow for the alchemy of art.'

However, they went off with an evident increase of comfort, founded on their demonstrable advantage in being the real thing. I could fancy them shuddering over Miss Churm. She was very droll about them when I went back, for I told her what they wanted.

'Well, if *she* can sit I'll tyke to book-keeping,' said my model.

'She's very lady-like,' I replied, as an innocent form of aggravation.

'So much the worse for *you*. That means she can't turn round.'

'She'll do for the fashionable novels.'

'Oh yes, she'll *do* for them!' my model humorously declared.

'Ain't they bad enough without her?' I had often sociably denounced them to Miss Churm.

prejudiced: discriminating. **distinguished**: important or famous. **charming**: fascinating. **so**: like this.

as near it: equally close to the subject wanted.

shabby: poor and vulgar. **allow**: consider.
alchemy: magic.
evident: obvious.
increase of comfort: happier state. **founded**: based. **demonstrable**: which could be shown. **the real thing**: really of a high social class. **fancy**: imagine. **shuddering**: feeling ill or shocked. **droll**: funny.
tyke: imitation of the London pronunciation of 'take'. **book-keeping**: accountancy, office-work.

aggravation: provocation.

turn round: move in the opposite direction.
do: be alright.
humorously: in an amused way.
declared: said.
Ain't: *(slang)* aren't. **sociably**: in a friendly way.
denounced: criticised.

3

It was for the elucidation of a mystery in one of these works that I first tried Mrs Monarch. Her husband came with her, to be useful if necessary - it was sufficiently clear that as a general thing he would prefer to come with her. At first I wondered if this were for 'propriety's' sake - if he were going to be jealous and meddling. The idea was too tiresome, and if it had been confirmed it would speedily have brought our acquaintance to a close. But I soon saw there was nothing in it and that if he accompanied Mrs Monarch it was (in addition to the chance of being wanted) simply because he had nothing else to do. When she was away from him his occupation was gone - she never *had* been away from him. I judged, rightly, that in their awkward situation their close union was their main comfort and that this union had no weak spot. It was a real marriage, an encouragement for the hesitating, a nut for pessimists to crack. Their address was humble (I remember afterwards thinking it had been the only thing about them that was really professional), and I could fancy the lamentable lodgings in which the Major would have been left alone. He could bear them with his wife - he couldn't bear them without her.

He had too much tact to try and make himself agreeable when he couldn't be useful; so he simply sat and waited, when I was too absorbed in my work to talk. But I liked to make him talk - it made my work, when it didn't interrupt

elucidation: clarification, solution. **these works**: the fashionable novels.

as a general thing: in general.
wondered: asked myself. **for 'propriety's' sake**: to avoid scandals. **jealous**: possessive about his wife. **meddling**: interfering. **tiresome**: boring. **speedily**: quickly.
brought our acquaintance to a close: finished our relationship.

chance: possibility. **wanted**: required.

occupation: way of passing the time.
judged: decided. **rightly**: correctly. **awkward**: difficult. **close**: intimate.
weak spot: place not as strong as others.
encouragement for the hesitating: stimulus to those people who could not decide to get married. **a nut for pessimists to crack**: people with negative views about marriage would find it difficult to criticise this one. **humble**: in a poor area. **fancy**: imagine. **lamentable**: poor. **lodgings**: house, rooms.
bear: tolerate.

tact: diplomacy. **agreeable**: pleasant.

absorbed in: concentrated on.

it, less sordid, less special. To listen to him was to combine the excitement of going out with the economy of staying at home. There was only one hindrance: that I seemed not to know any of the people he and his wife had known. I think he wondered extremely, during the term of our intercourse, whom the deuce I *did* know.

He hadn't a stray sixpence of an idea to fumble for; so we didn't spin it very fine - we confined ourselves to questions of leather and even of liquor (saddlers and breeches-makers and how to get good claret cheap), and matters like 'good trains' and the habits of small game. His lore on these last subjects was astonishing, he managed to interweave the stationmaster with the ornithologist. When he couldn't talk about greater things he could talk cheerfully about smaller, and since I couldn't accompany him into reminiscences of the fashionable world he could lower the conversation without a visible effort to my level.

So earnest a desire to please was touching in a man who could so easily have knocked one down. He looked after the fire and had an opinion on the draught of the stove, without my asking him, and I could see that he thought many of my arrangements not half clever enough. I remember telling him that if I were only rich I would offer him a salary to come and teach me how to live. Sometimes he gave a random sigh, of which the essence was: 'Give me even such a bare old barrack as *this*, and I'd do something with it!' When I wanted to use him he came alone; which was an illustration of the superior courage of women. His

sordid: squalid.

hindrance: problem.

wondered extremely: was very puzzled.
term of our intercourse: time of our relationship. **whom the deuce**: who on earth. **stray sixpence of an idea**: any idea at all. **fumble for**: find with difficulty. **spin it very fine**: talk about complicated or refined things. **confined**: limited. **leather**: material for shoes and other clothes, made from the skin of animals. **liquor**: alcoholic drinks. **saddlers**: people making accessories for horses. **breeches-makers**: people making trousers. **claret**: red wine. **cheap**: without spending much. **matters**: subjects. **small game**: small animals which were hunted. **lore**: knowledge, education. **astonishing**: very surprising. **managed to**: succeeded in. **interweave**: combine. **stationmaster**: man responsible for a railway station. **ornithologist**: person studying birds. **greater**: more important. **cheerfully**: happily. **since**: because. **reminiscences**: memories. **fashionable**: chic, in fashion. **lower**: take down. **a visible effort**: seen to be trying. **earnest**: sincere. **touching**: emotionally moving. **knocked one down**: hit someone. **draught of the stove**: how the heating worked. **arrangements**: organization. **half clever enough**: not very good.

random: without reason. **essence**: true quality.
bare: without much furniture or decoration. **barrack**: place where soldiers are accommodated.
illustration: show. **superior**: greater.

39

wife could bear her solitary second floor, and she was in general more discreet; showing by various small reserves that she was alive to the propriety of keeping our relations markedly professional - not letting them slide into sociability. She wished it to remain clear that she and the Major were employed, not cultivated, and if she approved of me as a superior, who could be kept in his place, she never thought me quite good enough for an equal.

She sat with great intensity, giving the whole of her mind to it, and was capable of remaining for an hour almost as motionless as if she were before a photographer's lens. I could see she had been photographed often, but somehow the very habit that made her good for that purpose unfitted her for mine. At first I was extremely pleased with her lady-like air, and it was a satisfaction, on coming to follow her lines, to see how good they were and how far they could lead the pencil. But after a few times I began to find her too insurmountably stiff; do what I would with it my drawing looked like a photograph or a copy of a photograph. Her figure had no variety of expression - she herself had no sense of variety. You may say that this was my business, was only a question of placing her. I placed her in every conceivable position, but she managed to obliterate their differences. She was always a lady certainly, and into the bargain was always the same lady. She was the real thing, but always the same thing. There were moments when I was oppressed by the serenity of her confidence that she *was* the real thing. All her dealings with me and all her

bear: tolerate. **solitary**: lonely, alone.
reserves: reserved behaviour.
alive to: conscious of. **propriety**: doing the socially acceptable thing. **markedly**: distinctly. **letting them slide**: letting them decline. **sociability**: a friendly relationship. **wished**: wanted. **cultivated**: kept as friends.

thought me: considered me.
sat: modelled. **the whole of her mind**: all her concentration.
capable of: able to.
motionless: without moving. **as if she were**: in a similar way to.
lens: glass piece of camera. **somehow**: in some way.
the very habit: exactly the habit.
unfitted her: made her unsuitable.
lady-like: high class. **air**: appearance.
follow her lines: draw her figure.
lead: guide.
insurmountably: in a way which was impossible to avoid. **stiff**: rigid. **do what I would with it**: whatever I did with it, note inversion.

placing her: putting her in the right position.
conceivable: imaginable. **managed to**: succeeded in. **obliterate**: destroy.
into the bargain: also, at the same time.

oppressed: made unhappy. **serenity**: tranquillity. **confidence**: being sure. **dealings**: relations.

41

husband's were an implication that this was lucky for *me*. Meanwhile I found myself trying to invent types that approached her own, instead of making her own transform itself - in the clever way that was not impossible, for instance, to poor Miss Churm. Arrange as I would and take the precautions I would, she always, in my pictures, came out too tall - landing me in the dilemma of having represented a fascinating woman as seven feet high, which, out of respect perhaps to my own very much scantier inches, was far from my idea of such a personage.

The case was worse with the Major - nothing I could do would keep *him* down, so that he became useful only for the representation of brawny giants. I adored variety and range, I cherished human accidents, the illustrative note; I wanted to characterize closely, and the thing in the world I most hated was the danger of being ridden by a type. I had quarrelled with some of my friends about it - I had parted company with them for maintaining that one *had* to be, and that if the type was beautiful (witness Raphael and Leonardo), the servitude was only a gain.

I was neither Leonardo nor Raphael; I might only be a presumptuous young modern searcher, but I held that everything was to be sacrificed sooner than character. When they averred that the haunting type in question could easily *be* character, I retorted, perhaps superficially: 'Whose?' It couldn't be everybody's - it might end in being nobody's. After I had drawn Mrs Monarch a dozen times I perceived more clearly than before that the value of such a model as

implication: indication.

Meanwhile: during this time.

approached: were nearer. **her own**: her own type.

clever: skilful, intelligent.

for instance: for example. **Arrange as I would**: however I organised. **take the precautions I would**: whatever precautions I took. **came out**: appeared. **landing me**: putting me. **dilemma**: impossible decision. **seven feet**: more than two metres.

scantier inches: lower height.

far from: not at all. **personage**: character.

brawny: strong and muscular. **giants**: enormous men. **adored**: loved. **range**: differences. **cherished**: loved. **illustrative note**: something unusual to draw. **characterize**: express the character of his models. **being ridden by a type**: having many of his paintings with the same type of characters. **quarrelled**: argued, disagreed. **parted company**: broken off a relationship. *had* **to be**: had to be ridden by a type. **witness**: see.

servitude: state of being forced to do something. **gain**: profit, positive advantage.

presumptuous: a little arrogant. **searcher**: someone looking for something. **held**: thought. **sooner than**: before.

averred: said, sustained. **haunting**: not leaving in peace.

retorted: said. **superficially**: without considering the matter deeply.

dozen: twelve. **perceived**: saw.

Miss Churm resided precisely in the fact that she had no positive stamp, combined of course with the other fact that what she did have was a curious and inexplicable talent for imitation. Her usual appearance was like a curtain which she could draw up at a request for a capital performance. This performance was simply suggestive; but it was a word to the wise - it was vivid and pretty. Sometimes, even, I thought it, though she was plain herself, too insipidly pretty; I made it a reproach to her that the figures drawn from her were monotonously (*bêtement*, as we used to say) graceful. Nothing made her more angry: it was so much her pride to feel that she could sit for characters that had nothing in common with each other. She would accuse me at such moments of taking away her 'reputytion'.

It suffered a certain shrinkage, this queer quality, from the repeated visits of my new friends. Miss Churm was greatly in demand, never in want of employment, so I had no scruple in putting her off occasionally, to try them more at my ease. It was certainly amusing at first to do the real thing - it was amusing to do Major Monarch's trousers. They *were* the real thing, even if he did come out colossal. It was amusing to do his wife's back hair (it was so mathematically neat) and the particular 'smart' tension of her tight stays. She lent herself especially to positions in which the face was somewhat averted or blurred; she abounded in ladylike back views and *profils perdus*. When she stood erect she took naturally one of the attitudes in which court painters represent queens and princesses; so

resided: lay, was.

stamp: character.

curious: strange. **inexplicable**: which could not be explained.

curtain: piece of cloth put over window or in the theatre.

draw up: move up, uncover. **capital**: excellent.

performance: show. **simply suggestive**: only suggested the real thing. **a word to the wise**: enough.

plain: not beautiful.

insipidly: without life. **reproach**: criticism.

monotonously: in a repetitive way. *bêtement:* French word, affected by artists. **graceful**: elegant.

sit: model.

'reputytion': imitation of London pronunciation of reputation.

shrinkage: decrease. **queer**: strange.

greatly in demand: always wanted for work. **in want of employment**: needing work. **scruple**: moral problem. **putting her off**: cancelling a session. **at my ease**: in a relaxed mood. **amusing**: enjoyable.

colossal: enormous.

neat: tidy, orderly. **'smart'**: elegant, in fashion.

tight: restricting. **stays**: invention to maintain a good figure. **lent herself**: was especially suitable. **averted**: turned away. **blurred**: not seen clearly. **abounded**: had lots of. **ladylike**: refined. **back views**: figure seen from back. *profils perdus: (French)* lost profiles. **erect**: straight. **court painters**: painters for Kings and Queens.

that I found myself wondering whether, to draw out this accomplishment, I couldn't get the editor of the *Cheapside* to publish a really royal romance, 'A Tale of Buckingham Palace'. Sometimes, however, the real thing and the make-believe came into contact; by which I mean that Miss Churm, keeping an appointment or coming to make one on days when I had much work in hand, encountered her invidious rivals. The encounter was not on their part, for they noticed her no more than if she had been the housemaid; not from intentional loftiness, but simply because, as yet, professionally, they didn't know how to fraternize as I could guess that they would have liked - or at least that the Major would. They couldn't talk about the omnibus - they always walked; and they didn't know what else to try - she wasn't interested in good trains or cheap claret. Besides, they must have felt - in the air - that she was amused at them, secretly derisive of their ever knowing how. She was not a person to conceal her scepticism if she had had a chance to show it. On the other hand Mrs Monarch didn't think her tidy; for why else did she take pains to say to me (it was going out of the way, for Mrs Monarch) that she didn't like dirty women ?

One day when my young lady happened to be present with my other sitters (she even dropped in, when it was convenient, for a chat), I asked her to be as good as to lend a hand in getting tea - a service with which she was familiar and which was one of a class that, living as I did in a small way, with slender domestic resources, I often appeal to my

wondering: asking myself, speculating. **whether**: if. **draw out**: use. **accomplishment**: skill, advantage. *Cheapside:* magazine.

make-believe: pretend, artificial.
keeping an appointment: comng at the right time.
much: a lot of. **encountered**: met.
invidious: jealous. **rivals**: people in competition with her.
noticed: observed, saw.
housemaid: servant. **loftiness**: sense of superiority.
as yet: until then. **fraternize**: make friends, behave sociably.

omnibus: public transport.
try: talk about.
cheap claret: inexpensive red wine.
Besides: in addition.
amused: laughing. **derisive**: making fun of.
knowing how: knowing how and why she found them funny.
conceal: hide. **scepticism**: state of not believing in something.
tidy: clean and well dressed.
take pains: try very hard. **going out of the way**: unusually explicit.
happened to be: was by chance.
sitters: models. **dropped in**: visited me
convenient: appropriate, possible. **chat**: friendly conversation.
as good as to lend a hand: it she would help.
class: type. **a small way**: with not much luxury.
slender: little. **domestic resources**: home comforts. **appeal to**: ask.

models to render. They liked to lay hands on my property, to break the sitting, and sometimes the china - I made them feel Bohemian. The next time I saw Miss Churm after this incident she surprised me greatly by making a scene about it - she accused me of having wished to humiliate her. She had not resented the outrage at the time, but had seemed obliging and amused, enjoying the comedy of asking Mrs Monarch, who sat vague and silent, whether she would have cream and sugar, and putting an exaggerated simper into the question. She had tried intonations - as if she too wished to pass for the real thing; till I was afraid my other visitors would take offence.

Oh, *they* were determined not to do this; and their touching patience was the measure of their great need. They would sit by the hour, uncomplaining, till I was ready to use them; they would come back on the chance of being wanted and would walk away cheerfully if they were not. I used to go to the door with them to see in what magnificent order they retreated. I tried to find other employment for them - I introduced them to several artists. But they didn't 'take', for reasons I could appreciate, and I became conscious, rather anxiously, that after such disappointments they fell back upon me with a heavier weight. They did me the honour to think that it was I who was most *their* form. They were not picturesque enough for the painters, and in those days there were not so many serious workers in black and white. Besides, they had an eye to the great job I had mentioned to them - they had secretly set their hearts on sup-

lay hands: touch.

break the sitting: interrupt the mdellling session. **the china**: the cups and plates, note pun on break. **Bohemian**: alternative.

making a scene: arguing.

wished: wanted. **humiliate**: put in an embarrassing position.

resented: minded. **outrage**: insult.

obliging: helpful.

vague: unclear. **whether**: if.

simper: insincere sound.

intonations: tones of voice.

wished: wanted. **pass**: be accepted as.

take offence: be offended.

touching: emotionally moving.

was the measure of: corresponded to.

by the hour: for hours. **uncomplaining**: without saying anything.

cheerfully: happily.

magnificent: splendid.

retreated: went back.

'take': have any success.

appreciate: realise, understand.

rather: quite. **anxiously**: in a worried way.

fell back upon me: came and modelled for me.

picturesque: pretty and interesting.

had an eye to: were thinking about.
mentioned to them: told them about. **set their hearts**: had the ambition.

plying the right essence for my pictorial vindication of our fine novelist. They knew that for this undertaking I should want no costume-effects, none of the frippery of past ages - that it was a case in which everything would be contemporary and satirical and, presumably, genteel. If I could work them into it their future would be assured, for the labour would of course be long and the occupation steady. One day Mrs Monarch came without her husband - she explained his absence by his having had to go to the City. While she sat there in her usual anxious stiffness there came, at the door, a knock which I immediately recognized as the subdued appeal of a model out of work. It was followed by the entrance of a young man whom I easily perceived to be a foreigner and who proved in fact an Italian acquainted with no English word but my name, which he uttered in a way that made it seem to include all others. I had not then visited his country, nor was I proficient in his tongue; but as he was not so meanly constituted - what Italian is? - as to depend only on that member for expression he conveyed to me, in familiar but graceful mimicry, that he was in search of exactly the employment in which the lady before me was engaged. I was not struck with him at first, and while I continued to draw I emitted rough sounds of discouragement

and dismissal. He stood his ground, however, not importunately, but with a dumb, dog-like fidelity in his eyes which amounted to innocent impudence - the manner of a devoted servant (he might have been in the house for

right essence: correct quality. **pictorial**: illustrated. **vindication**: saving the reputation of. **fine**: good. **novelist**: person writing novels. **undertaking**: enterprise, job. **frippery**: frivolity, complications.

contemporary: of the present day. **satirical**: a comic attack on abuse or bad habits. **genteel**: high-class. **work them into it**: find the opportunity for them to participate. **assured**: guaranteed. **labour**: work. **steady**: stable, constant.

anxious: worried. **stiffness**: rigidity, inflexibility.
knock: sound of someone at door.
subdued: soft. **appeal**: request.

perceived: saw, understood. **proved**: was.
acquainted with: knowing. **but**: apart from.
uttered: said.

proficient in: good at. **tongue**: language. **meanly**: poorly. **consituted**: formed.
that member: the tongue, used for speaking. **conveyed**: communicated. **graceful**: elegant. **mimicry**: gesture. **in search of**: looking for. **engaged**: busy, occupied.
not struck with: not enthusiastic about.
emitted: made. **rough**: aggressive.
dismissal: to send him away. **stood his ground**: stayed where he was. **importunately**: aggressively. **dumb**: not speaking. **dog-like**: similar to a dog. **fidelity**: trust. **amounted to**: constituted. **impudence**: rudeness. **devoted**: dedicated.

years) unjustly suspected. Suddenly I saw that this very attitude and expression made a picture, whereupon I told him to sit down and wait till I should be free. There was another picture in the way he obeyed me, and I observed as I worked that there were others still in the way he looked wonderingly, with his head thrown back, about the high studio. He might have been crossing himself in St Peter's. Before I finished I said to myself: 'The fellow's a bankrupt orange-monger, but he's a treasure.'

When Mrs Monarch withdrew he passed across the room like a flash to open the door for her, standing there with the rapt, pure gaze of the young Dante spellbound by the young Beatrice. As I never insisted, in such situations, on the blankness of the British domestic, I reflected that he had the making of a servant (and I needed one, but couldn't pay him to be only that), as well as of a model; in short I made up my mind to adopt my bright adventurer if he would agree to officiate in the double capacity. He jumped at my offer, and in the event my rashness (for I had known nothing about him) was not brought home to me. He proved a sympathetic though a desultory ministrant, and had in a wonderful degree *the sentiment de la pose*. It was uncultivated, instinctive; a part of the happy instinct which had guided him to my door and helped him to spell out my name on the card nailed to it. He had had no other introduction to me than a guess, from the shape of my high north window, seen outside, that my place was a studio and that as a studio it would contain an artist. He had wandered to

unjustly: unfairly.

this very attitude: precisely this attitude. **whereupon**: at which moment. **till I should be free**: until I was free.

obeyed me: did what I told him.

others still: even more pictures.

wonderingly: in surprise.

crossing himself: making a religious gesture, the sign of the cross. **St Peter's**: St. Peter's in the Vatican City. **bankrupt**: without money. **orange-monger**: person selling oranges. **treasure**: delightful person, valuable person. **withdrew**: went out.

flash: something very quick.

rapt: absorbed. **gaze**: look. **spellbound**: entranced, completely fascinated.

blankness: lack of emotion and character.

making of a servant: potential to be a good servant.

in short: in a few words.

bright: luminous, intelligent. **adventurer**: person taking risks.

officiate: do his duty. **double capacity**: servant and model.

jumped at: took immediately. **in the event**: in this case. **rashness**: hurried decision. **was not brought home to me**: did not make me suffer. **sympathetic**: compassionate. **desultory**: superficial. **ministrant**: servant. **degree**: extent. *sentiment de la pose: (French)* right feeling for modelling. **uncultivated**: uneducated. **instinctive**: without thinking.

nailed: attached with a piece of metal.

guess: speculation. **shape**: form.

wandered: come without planning it.

England in search of fortune, like other itinerants, and had embarked, with a partner and a small green handcart, on the sale of penny ices. The ices had melted away and the partner had dissolved in their train. My young man wore tight yellow trousers with reddish stripes and his name was Oronte. He was sallow but fair, and when I put him into some old clothes of my own he looked like an Englishman. He was as good as Miss Churm, who could look, when required, like an Italian.

4

I thought Mrs Monarch's face slightly convulsed when, on her coming back with her husband, she found Oronte installed.

It was strange to have to recognize in a scrap of a *lazzarone* a competitor to her magnificent Major. It was she who scented danger first, for the Major was anecdotically unconscious. But Oronte gave us tea, with a hundred eager confusions (he had never seen such a queer process), and I think she thought better of me for having at last an 'establishment'. They saw a couple of drawings that I had made of the establishment, and Mrs Monarch hinted that it never would have struck her that he had sat for them. 'Now the drawings you make from *us*, they look exactly like us,' she reminded me, smiling in triumph; and I recognized that this was indeed just their defect. When I

in search of fortune: looking for money and fame. **itinerants**: people not living and working in one place. **embarked on**: tried, risked. **handcart**: kind of travelling vehicle to sell things. **penny ices**: ice creams costing one penny. **melted away**: disappeared, become liquid. **dissolved**: disappeared, become liquid. **in their train**: following them. **tight**: close-fitting, restricted. **reddish stripes**: vertical lines of a red colour. **sallow**: with a dark skin. **fair**: with blonde hair.

slightly: a little. **convulsed**: distorted.

installed: established.
scrap: small creature or piece. *lazzarone:* poor person from the street, living by his intelligence *(Italian)*.
scented: detected, noticed. **anecdotically**: by the telling of stories. **eager**: enthusiastic.
queer: strange.

'establishment': a proper home *(with servants)*.
hinted: suggested.
it never would have struck her: she would never have thought.
sat: modelled.
reminded: told. **triumph**: victory.
indeed: really. **just**: precisely. **defect**: disadvantage.

drew the Monarchs I couldn't, somehow, get away from them - get into the character I wanted to represent; and I had not the least desire my model should be discoverable in my picture. Miss Churm never was, and Mrs Monarch thought I hid her, very properly because she was vulgar; whereas if she was lost it was only as the dead who go to heaven are lost - in the gain of an angel the more.

By this time I had got a certain start with *Rutland Ramsay,* the first novel in the great projected series; that is I had produced a dozen drawings, several with the help of the Major and his wife, and I had sent them in for approval. My understanding with the publishers, as I have already hinted, had been that I was to be left to do my work, in this particular case, as I liked, with the whole book committed to me; but my connexion with the rest of the series was only contingent. There were moments when, frankly, it *was* a comfort to have the real thing under one's hand; for there were characters in *Rutland Ramsay* that were very much like it. There were people presumably as straight as the Major and women of as good a fashion as Mrs Monarch. There was a great deal of country-house life - treated, it is true, in a fine, fanciful, ironical, generalized way - and there was a considerable implication of knickerbockers and kilts. There were certain things I had to settle at the outset; such things for instance as the exact appearance of the hero, the particular bloom of the heroine. The author of course gave me a lead, but there was a margin for interpretation. I took the Monarchs into my confidence, I told them

somehow: in some way. **get away**: escape.
get into: enter.
discoverable: could be seen.

hid: concealed. **properly**: correctly.
whereas: but, while.
heaven: paradise. **gain**: advantage. **an angel the more**: an extra angel. **got a certain start**: made some progress.
projected: planned.
dozen: twelve. **several**: some of them.
approval: consideration.
understanding: agreement.
hinted: suggested.
committed: given by contract.
connexion: link.
was only contingent: depended on circumstances. **frankly**: honestly. **to have the real thing under one's hand**: to be dealing with the real thing.
presumably: I suppose. **straight**: rigid, formal.

treated: written about.
fanciful: imaginative. **ironical**: humorous.
implication: involvement. **knickerbockers**: trousers ending at the knee. **kilts**: clothes worn by Scotsmen. **settle**: establish.
outset: beginning.
bloom: appearance of the face and skin. **heroine**: female protagonist. **gave me a lead**: helped me, gave me some indications.
margin: room, space. **took the Monarchs into my confidence**: told the Monarchs about it.

frankly what I was about, I mentioned my embarrassments and alternatives. 'Oh, take *him*!' Mrs Monarch murmured sweetly, looking at her husband; and 'What could you want better than my wife?' the Major inquired, with the comfortable candour that now prevailed between us.

I was not obliged to answer these remarks - I was only obliged to place my sitters. I was not easy in mind, and I postponed, a little timidly perhaps, the solution of the question. The book was a large canvas, the other figures were numerous, and I worked off at first some of the episodes in which the hero and the heroine were not concerned. When once I had set *Them* up I should have to stick to them - I couldn't make my young man seven feet high in one place and five feet nine in another. I inclined on the whole to the latter measurements, though the major more than once reminded me that *he* looked about as young as anyone. It was indeed quite impossible to arrange him, for the figure, so that it would have been difficult to detect his age. After the spontaneous Oronte had been with me a month, and after I had given him to understand several different times that his native exuberance would presently constitute an insurmountable barrier to our further intercourse, I waked to a sense of his heroic capacity. He was only five feet seven, but the remaining inches were latent. I tried him almost secretly at first, for I was really rather afraid of the judgement my other models would pass on such a choice. If they regarded Miss Churm as little better than a snare, what would they think of the representation

was about: was doing.
murmured: said softly.

candour: honesty. **prevailed**: usually occurred.

easy in mind: relaxed, satisfied,.
postponed: delayed, changed to a later date.
canvas: material for an oil painting.
worked off: completed.

set *Them* up: created a figure for the hero and heroine.
stick to them: keep them as they were. **seven feet**: more than two metres. **five feet nine**: about 175 cm. **inclined**: preferred.
on the whole: in general. **latter measurements**: five feet nine.

arrange: organize.
detect: discover, know.

given him to understand: communicated to him.
exuberance: high spirits, exaggeration. **presently**: soon.
consitute: form. **barrier**: limit.
intercourse: relationship. **waked to**: realised.
five feet seven. about 170 cm. **inches**: measure of length in England, 1 inch = 2.5 cm. **latent**: potential.

little better than a snare: not much more than a trap.

by a person so little the real thing as an Italian street-vendor of a protagonist formed by a public school?

If I went a little in fear of them it was not because they bullied me, because they had got an oppressive foothold, but because in their really pathetic decorum and mysteriously permanent newness they counted on me so intensely. I was therefore very glad when Jack Hawley came home: he was always of such good counsel. He painted badly himself, but there was no one like him for putting his finger on the place. He had been absent from England for a year; he had been somewhere - I don't remember where - to get a fresh eye. I was in a good deal of dread of any such organ, but we were old friends; he had been away for months and a sense of emptiness was creeping into my life. I hadn't dodged a missile for a year.

He came back with a fresh eye, but with the same old black velvet blouse, and the first evening he spent in my studio we smoked cigarettes till the small hours. He had done no work himself, he had only got the eye; so the field was clear for the production of my little things. He wanted to see what I had done for the *Cheapside*, but he was disappointed in the exhibition. That at least seemed the meaning of two or three comprehensive groans which, as he lounged on my big divan, on a folded leg, looking at my latest drawings, issued from his lips with the smoke of the cigarette.

'What's the matter with you?' I asked.

'What's the matter with *you*?'

'Nothing save that I'm mystified.'

street-vendor: someone who sells things in the street.

protagonist formed by a public school: hero educated in one of the best schools in England. **If I went a little in fear of them**: if I acted under their influence. **bullied**: treated badly. **foothold**: position. **decorum**: good behaviour.

counted on: relied on.

therefore: for this reason.

good counsel: gave me good advice.

putting his finger on the place: identifying the problem.

get a fresh eye: have a new vision of things. **a good deal of**: a lot of. **dread**: fear. **any such organ**: a fresh eye.
emptiness: being without a vital component of life. **creeping**: coming slowly. **dodged a missile**: avoided a difficult comment.

velvet: soft material. **blouse**: type of shirt.
the small hours: early in the morning.
field was clear: there was an opportunity.

Cheapside: an English magazine of the time.
disappointed: not satisfied.
comprehensive: large, including everything. **groans**: unhappy sounds. **lounged**: lay. **folded**: sitting on one leg. **latest**: most recent. **issued**: came out.

save: apart from. **I'm mystified**: I can't understand at all.

'You are indeed. You're quite off the hinge. What's the meaning of this new fad?' And he tossed me, with visible irreverence, a drawing in which I happened to have depicted both my majestic models. I asked if he didn't think it good, and he replied that it struck him as execrable, given the sort of thing I had always represented myself to him as wishing to arrive at; but I let that pass, I was so anxious to see exactly what he meant. The two figures in the picture looked colossal, but I supposed this was *not* what he meant, inasmuch as, for aught he knew to the contrary, I might have been trying for that. I maintained that I was working exactly in the same way as when he last had done me the honour to commend me. ' Well, there's a big hole somewhere,' he answered; 'wait a bit and I'll discover it.' I depended upon him to do so: where else was the fresh eye? But he produced at last nothing more luminous than 'I don't know - I don't like your types.' This was lame, for a critic who had never consented to discuss with me anything but the question of execution, the direction of strokes, and the mystery of values.

'In the drawings you've been looking at I think my types are very handsome.'

'Oh, they won't do!'

'I've had a couple of new models.'

'I see you have. *They* won't do.'

'Are you very sure of that?'

'Absolutely - they're stupid.'

'You mean *I* am - for I ought to get round that.'

indeed: really. **quite off the hinge**: completely mad.

fad: silly fashion. **tossed**: threw.

irreverence: without respect. **happened**: had by chance.

both my majestic models: Mr and Mrs Monarch.

struck him as execrable: seemed terrible to him.

represented myself to him: told him.

wishing: wanting. **let that pass**: accepted that. **anxious**: worried.

colossal: enormous.

inasmuch: because. **aught**: anything.

maintained: argued.

commend me: say nice things about my work.

a bit: a little.

luminous: informative.

types: models, types of character. **lame**: not very convincing.

but: apart from. **execution**: technical aspect of painting. **strokes**: how the brush is moved when painting.

handsome: good-looking.

won't do: are not acceptable.

ought to: should. **get round that**: avoid the problem.

'You *can't* - with such people. Who are they?'

I told him, as far as was necessary, and he declared, heartlessly: '*Ce sont des gens qu'il faut mettre à la porte.*'

'You've never seen them; they're awfully good,' I compassionately objected.

'Not seen them. Why, all this recent work of yours drops to pieces with them. It's all I want to see of them.'

'No one else has said anything against it - the *Cheapside* people are pleased.'

'Everyone else is an ass, and the *Cheapside* people the biggest asses of all. Come, don't pretend, at this time of day, to have pretty illusions about the public, especially about publishers and editors. It's not for *such* animals you work - it's for those who know, *coloro che sanno*; so keep straight for *me* if you can't keep straight for yourself. There's a certain sort of thing you tried for from the first - and a very good thing it is. But this twaddle isn't *in* it.'

When I talked with Hawley later about *Rutland Ramsay* and its possible successors he declared that I must get back into my boat again or I would go to the bottom. His voice in short was the voice of warning.

I noted the warning, but I didn't turn my friends out of doors. They bored me a good deal; but the very fact that they bored me admonished me not to sacrifice them - if there was anything to be done with them - simply to irritation. As I look back at this phase they seem to me to have pervaded my life not a little. I have a vision of them as most of the time in my studio, seated, against the wall,

declared: said.

heartlessly: without emotion, cruelly. *'Ce sont des gens qu'il faut mettre à' la porte'*: (French) These are people to be thrown out. **awfully**: terribly. **compassionately**: with sympathy for the Monarchs.

drops to pieces: falls apart, is destroyed.

Cheapside: English magazine of the time.

an ass: very stupid.

pretend: deceive yourself.

at this time of day: at this point in your career. **pretty**: elegant.

coloro che sanno: the people who know *(Italian)*.

keep straight: be honest.

from the first: from the beginning.

twaddle: nonsense, poor quality work.

successors: following volumes. **declared**: said.

get back into my boat again: return to my previous style. **go to the bottom**: sink, fail. **in short**: in a few words. **warning**: serious advice.

very fact: exactly the fact.

admonished: warned

phase: period.

pervaded: filled.

seated: sitting down.

on an old velvet bench to be out of the way, and looking like a pair of patient courtiers in a royal antechamber. I am convinced that during the coldest weeks of the winter they held their ground because it saved them fire. Their newness was losing its gloss, and it was impossible not to feel that they were objects of charity. Whenever Miss Churm arrived they went away, and after I was fairly launched in *Rutland Ramsay* Miss Churm arrived pretty often. They managed to express to me tacitly that they supposed I wanted her for the low life of the book, and I let them suppose it, since they had attempted to study the work - it was lying about the studio - without discovering that it dealt only with the highest circles. They had dipped into the most brilliant of our novelists without deciphering many passages. I still took an hour from them, now and again, in spite of Jack Hawley's warning: it would be time enough to dismiss them, if dismissal should be necessary, when the rigour of the season was over. Hawley had made their acquaintance - he had met them at my fireside - and thought them a ridiculous pair. Learning that he was a painter they tried to approach him, to show him too that they were the real thing; but he looked at them, across the big room, as if they were miles away: they were a compendium of everything that he most objected to in the social system of his country. Such people
as that, all convention and patent-leather, with ejaculations that stopped conversation, had no business in a studio. A studio was a place to learn to see, and how could you see through a pair of feather beds?

velvet: kind of soft material. **bench**: kind of long seat.

courtiers: people from the King or Queen's circle. **antechamber**: room, where one waited to talk to a monarch.

held their ground: stayed in the studio. **saved them fire**: they didn't use fuel. **gloss**: shining surface.

objects of charity: something to feel sorry for.

fairly launched: quite involved.

pretty: quite.

managed: succeeded. **tacitly**: silently.

low life: vulgar characters.

lying about: positioned around. **discovering**: finding out.

dealt with: treated. **the highest circles**: the upper classes.

dipped into: read a little of. **deciphering**: understanding.

in spite of: ignoring.

dismiss them: terminate their employment.

rigour: hard work.

made their acquaintance: met them. **at my fireside**: in front of my fire, in my living room.

approach him: make friends with him.

miles away: very distant.

compendium: collection. **objected to**: hated.

convention: social tradition. **patent-leather**: expensive material for making shoes. **ejaculations**: sudden exclamations. **had no business**: had nothing to do, were out of place.

feather beds: mattresses.

The main inconvenience I suffered at their hands was that, at first, I was shy of letting them discover how my artful little servant had begun to sit for me for *Rutland Ramsay*. They knew that I had been odd enough (they were prepared by this time to allow oddity to artists) to pick a foreign vagabond out of the streets, when I might have had a person with whiskers and credentials; but it was some time before they learned how high I rated his accomplishments. They found him in an attitude more than once, but they never doubted I was doing him as an organ-grinder. There were several things they never guessed, and one of them was that for a striking scene in the novel, in which a footman briefly figured, it occurred to me to make use of Major Monarch as the menial. I kept putting this off, I didn't like to ask him to don the livery - besides the difficulty of finding a livery to fit him. At last, one day late in the winter, when I was at work on the despised Oronte (he caught one's idea in an instant), and was in the glow of feeling that I was going very straight, they came in, the Major and his wife, with their society laugh about nothing (there was less and less to laugh at), like country-callers - they always reminded me of that - who have walked across the park after church and are presently persuaded to stay to luncheon. Luncheon was over, but they could stay to tea - I knew they wanted it. The fit was on me, however, and I couldn't let my ardour cool and my work wait, with the fading daylight, while my model prepared it. So I asked Mrs Monarch if she would mind laying it out - a request

letting them discover: allowing them to know. **artful**: cunning. clever. **sit**: model.

odd: strange.

oddity: strangeness.

pick… out: choose. **vagabond**: person not living in a fixed place.

whiskers: facial hair. **credentials**: references from other people.

rated: considered. **accomplishments**: skills.

attitude: pose.

organ-grinder: street-musician.

striking: exciting, powerful.

footman: servant. **briefly**: for a short time. **figured**: appeared.

it occurred to me: I thought. **menial**: servant. **putting this off**: delaying the moment until later. **don**: put on. **livery**: servant's uniform. **besides**: apart from.

despised: hated.

caught one's idea: understood one.

glow of feeling: excitement. **straight**: well.

society laugh: conventional laugh.

country-callers: people visiting rich homes in the country.

presently: soon.

fit: desire to work, inspiration.

ardour: enthusiasm. **cool**: decline.

fading: getting darker.

mind: object. **laying it out**: preparing it.

which, for an instant, brought all the blood to her face. Her eyes were on her husband's for a second, and some mute telegraphy passed between them. Their folly was over the next instant; his cheerful shrewdness put an end to it. So far from pitying their wounded pride, I must add, I was moved to give it as complete a lesson as I could. They bustled about together and got out the cups and saucers and made the kettle boil. I know they felt as if they were waiting on my servant, and when the tea was prepared I said: 'He'll have a cup, please - he's tired.' Mrs Monarch brought him one where he stood, and he took it from her as if he had been a gentleman at a party, squeezing a crush-hat with an elbow.

Then it came over me that she had made a great effort for me - made it with a kind of nobleness - and that I owed her a compensation. Each time I saw her after this I wondered what the compensation could be. I couldn't go on doing the wrong thing to oblige them. Oh, it *was* the wrong thing, the stamp of the work for which they sat - Hawley was not the only person to say it now. I sent in a large number of the drawings I had made for *Rutland Ramsay*, and I received a warning that was more to the point than Hawley's. The artistic adviser of the house for which I was working was of opinion that many of my illustrations were not what had been looked for. Most of these illustrations were the subjects in which the Monarchs had figured. Without going into the question of what *had* been looked for, I saw at this rate I shouldn't get the other books to do. I hurled myself

brought all the blood to her face: made her red with embarrassment. **mute:** without speaking.

folly: madness. **over:** finished.

instant: moment. **cheerful:** happy. **shrewdness:** cunning, intelligent behaviour. **So far from pitying:** I did not pity at all.

wounded: hurt, damaged. **moved:** stimulated. **bustled:** moved busily. **saucers:** little plates put under cups.

kettle: for boiling water. **waiting on:** serving.

squeezing: putting pressure on. **crush-hat:** a soft hat which can be collapsed. **elbow:** joint in arm.

it came over me: I began to think. **effort:** attempt.

owed: was obliged to give.

go on: continue.

stamp: character. **sat:** modelled.

more to the point: more direct.

adviser: counsellor, expert. **house:** publishing house.

was of opinion: thought.

figured: appeared.

going into: examining.

at this rate: at this rhythm of working. **hurled:** threw.

in despair upon Miss Churm, I put her through all her paces. I not only adopted Oronte publicly as my hero, but one morning when the Major looked in to see if I didn't require him to finish a figure for the *Cheapside*, for which he had begun to sit the week before, I told him that I had changed my mind - I would do the drawing from my man. At this my visitor turned pale and stood looking at me. 'Is *he* your idea of an English gentleman?' he asked.

I was disappointed, I was nervous, I wanted to get on with my work; so I replied with irritation: 'Oh, my dear Major - I can't be ruined for *you*!'

He stood another moment; then, without a word, he quitted the studio. I drew a long breath when he was gone, for I said to myself that I shouldn't see him again. I had not told him definitely that I was in danger of having my work rejected, but I was vexed at his not having felt the catastrophe in the air, read with me the moral of our fruitless collaboration, the lesson that, in the deceptive atmosphere of art, even the highest respectability may fail of being plastic.

I didn't owe my friends money, but I did see them again. They re-appeared together, three days later, and under the circumstances there was something tragic in the fact. It was a proof to me that they could find nothing else in life to do. They had threshed the matter out in a dismal conference - they had digested the bad news that they were not in for the series. If they were not useful to me even for the *Cheapside* their function seemed difflcult to determine, and I could only judge at first that they had come, forgivin-

despair: desperation, state of being without hope.

put her through all her paces: made her do all the different characters she knew. **looked in**: visited.

Cheapside: English magazine of the time.

sit: model.

my man: my servant.

get on: make progress.

ruined: face financial disaster.

quitted: left.

drew a long breath: respired deeply.

rejected: refused.

vexed: annoyed, irritated. **catastrophe**: disaster.

read with me: seen with me. **fruitless**: sterile, useless.

deceptive: tricky, misleading.

respectability: social convention. **fail of being plastic**: not be attractive to the eye. **owe**: need to give.

proof: evidence.

threshed the matter out: discussed everything. **dismal**: depressing **conference**: discussion. **digested**: accepted.

determine: decide.

gly, decorously, to take a last leave. This made me rejoice in secret that I had little leisure for a scene; for I had placed both my other models in position together and I was pegging away at a drawing from which I hoped to derive glory. It had been suggested by the passage in which Rutland Ramsay, drawing up a chair to Artemisia's piano-stool, says extraordinary things to her while she ostensibly fingers out a difficult piece of music. I had done Miss Churm at the piano before - it was an attitude in which she knew how to take on an absolutely poetic grace. I wished the two figures to 'compose' together, intensely, and my little Italian had entered perfectly into my conception. The pair were vividly before me, the piano had been pulled out; it was a charming picture of blended youth and murmured love, which I had only to catch and keep. My visitors stood and looked at it, and I was friendly to them over my shoulder.

They made no response, but I was used to silent company and went on with my work, only a little disconcerted (even though exhilarated by the sense that *this* was at last the ideal thing) at not having got rid of them after all. Presently I heard Mrs Monarch's sweet voice beside, or rather above me: 'I wish her hair was a little better done.' I looked up and she was staring with a strange fixedness at Miss Churm, whose back was turned to her. 'Do you mind my just touching it?' she went on - a question which made me spring up for an instant, as with the instinctive fear that she might do the young lady a harm. But she quieted me with

forgivingly: without rancour. **decorously**: politely. **take a last leave**: say goodbye for ever. **leisure**: free time. **for**: because.

pegging: working. **derive**: get.
passage: piece of text.
drawing up: moving, bringing near.
piano-stool: seat for playing the piano. **ostensibly**: plausibly, supposedly. **fingers out**: tries.
attitude: position.
grace: attractive appearance. **wished**: wanted.

conception: idea.
vividly: as in real life. **before me**: in front of me.
charming: lovely. **blended**: mixed, combined. **murmured**: said in a low voice. **catch**: *(here)* paint.

over my shoulder: without turning round.
response: answer.
disconcerted: worried.
though: if. **exhilarated**: excited.
got rid of them: disposed of them, excluded them.

staring: looking. **fixedness**: immobility.

just: only.
spring up: get up suddenly. **instant**: moment.
harm: hurt, damage. **quieted**: tranquillized.

a glance I shall never forget - I confess I should like to have been able to paint *that* - and went for a moment to my model. She spoke to her softly, laying a hand upon her shoulder and bending over her; and as the girl, understanding, gratefully assented, she disposed her rough curls, with a few quick passes, in such a way as to make Miss Churm's head twice as charming. It was one of the most heroic personal services I have ever seen rendered. Then Mrs Monarch turned away with a low sigh and, looking about her as if for something to do, stooped to the floor with a noble humility and picked up a dirty rag that had dropped out of my paint-box.

The Major meanwhile had also been looking for something to do and, wandering to the other end of the studio, saw before him my breakfast things, neglected, unremoved. 'I say, can't I be useful *here*?' he called out to me with an irrepressible quaver.

I assented with a laugh that I fear was awkward and for the next ten minutes, while I worked, I heard the light clatter of china and the tinkle of spoons and glass. Mrs Monarch assisted her husband - they washed up my crockery, they put it away. They wandered off into my little scullery, and I afterwards found that they had cleaned my knives and that my slender stock of plate had an unprecedented surface. When it came over me, the latent eloquence of what they were doing, I confess that my drawing was blurred for a moment - the picture swam. They had accepted their failure, but they couldn't accept their fate. They had

glance: look. **confess**: admit.

that: the look.

laying: putting.

shoulder: upper part of back. **bending**: curving.

gratefully: with thanks. **assented**: agreed. **disposed**: organized. **rough**: not fine or soft. **curls**: circles of hair. **passes**: movements. **charming**: pretty.

rendered: done.

sigh: sound of regret, of sadness.

stooped: went down.

humility: simplicity. **rag**: piece of cloth for cleaning.

paint-box: box containing paints etc.

wandering: moving without a particular purpose.

neglected: left without attention.

unremoved: not put away.

irrepressible: which he could not control. **quaver**: trembling in his voice. **assented**: agreed. **fear**: am afraid. **awkward**: not elegant. **clatter**: sound of plates.

china: plates and cups. **tinkle**: sound of metal or glass.

assisted: helped. **crockery**: cups and plates.

wandered off: went away. **scullery**: small room near kitchen.

slender: small. **stock**: collection. **plate**: silver dishes. **unprecedented**: never seen before. **surface**: shine. **it came over me**: I realised. **latent**: not stated. **eloquence**: expressiveness. **confess**: admit. **blurred**: unclear. **swam**: moved in front of my eyes. **fate**: destiny.

bowed their heads in bewilderment to the perverse and cruel law in virtue of which the real thing could be so much less precious than the unreal; but they didn't want to starve. If my servants were my models, my models might be my servants. They would reverse the parts - the others would sit for the ladies and gentlemen, and *they* would do the work. They would still be in the studio - it was an intense dumb appeal to me not to turn them out. 'Take us on,' they wanted to say - 'we'll do *anything*.'

When all this hung before me the *afflatus* vanished - my pencil dropped from my hand. My sitting was spoiled and I got rid of my sitters, who were also evidently rather mystified and awestruck. Then, alone with the Major and his wife, I had a most uncomfortable moment. He put their prayer into a single sentence: 'I say, you know - just let *us* do for you, can't you?'

I couldn't - it was dreadful to see them emptying my slops; but I pretended I could to oblige them for about a week. Then I gave them a sum of money to go away; and I never saw them again. I obtained the remaining books, but my friend Hawley repeats that Major and Mrs Monarch did me a permanent harm, got me into a second-rate trick. If it be true I am content to have paid the price - for the memory.

bowed: moved down in humility. **bewilderment**: not understanding. **perverse**: unnatural. **in virtue of which**: because of which. **precious**: valuable. **starve**: die of hunger.

reverse: invert.
sit: model.

dumb: without speaking. **appeal**: request. **turn them out**: throw them out.
hung before me: was before my eyes. *afflatus:* inspiration. **vanished**: disappeared. **dropped**: fell. **sitting**: artistic session. **spoiled**: ruined. **got rid of**: told to go away. **sitters**: models. **evidently**: obviously. **mystified**: perplexed. **awestruck**: didn't know what to say or do.

do: work, serve.
dreadful: terrible. **emptying my slops**: throwing away what food he left. **oblige them**: do this for them.
sum: quantity.
obtained: got.

harm: damage. **second-rate**: second-class, inferior. **trick**: type of work. **content**: satisfied, happy.

EASY READERS – ACTIVITY BOOKS

Defoe	ROBINSON CRUSOE
Dickens	A CHRISTMAS CAROL
James	GHOST STORIES
Kipling	JUNGLE BOOK STORIES
London	THE CALL OF THE WILD
Naudi	RUN FOR IT!
Stevenson	THE STRANGE CASE OF DR. JEKYLL AND MR. HYDE
Swift	GULLIVER'S TRAVELS
Twain	THE ADVENTURES OF TOM SAWYER
	ROBIN HOOD STORIES

MEISTERE DEIN DEUTSCH

Büchner	LEONCE UND LENA
Grimm	AUSGEWÄHLTE MÄRCHEN (Der Wolf und die sieben jungen Geißlein, Hänsel und Gretel, Aschenputtel, Sneewitt chen)
Hoffmann	SPIELERGLÜCK
Kafka	IN DER STRAFKOLONIE
Keller	DIE DREI GERECHTEN KAMMACHER
Schnitzler	DIE TOTEN SCHWEIGEN, Das Tagebuch der Redegonda, Die Braut
Storm	IMMENSEE
Wedekind	DAS OPFERLAMM, Die Liebe auf den ersten Blick, Die Schutzimpfung, Bella, Rabbi Esra

AMÉLIORE TON FRANÇAIS

Balzac	NAPOLEON DU PEUPLE, El Verdugo
Flaubert	UN CŒUR SIMPLE
La Fontaine	FABLES
Maupassant	LE PETIT FÛT, Au Bois, Le Testament, Le Baptême, Le Gâteau, Le Creusot, La Relique
Molière	L'AMOUR MÉDECIN
Molière	LES PRÉCIEUSES RIDICULES
Rousseau	RÊVERIES DU PROMENEUR SOLITAIRE
Stendhal	LES CENCI
Voltaire	MICROMÉGAS, Le monde comme il va